THE **NINJAGO** MOVIE

D0197429

LORD
GARMADON'S
GUIDE TO
WORLD
DOMINATION

BY
MEREDITH RUSU

SCHOLASTIC INC.

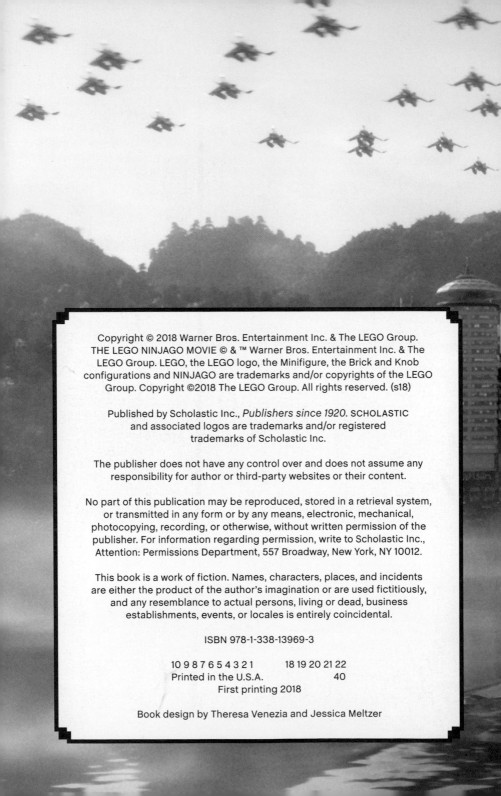

Published by Scholastic Inc., *Publishers since 1920*. SCHOLASTIC
and associated logos are trademarks and/or registered
trademarks of Scholastic Inc.

ISBN 978-1-338-13969-3

10 9 8 7 6 5 4 3 2 1   18 19 20 21 22
Printed in the U.S.A.   40
First printing 2018

Book design by Theresa Venezia and Jessica Meltzer

CONTENTS

LET'S GET THIS
CONQUERING
PARTY
STARTED!

INTRODUCTION

Oh, hello. Didn't see you there. The name's Garmadon. As in, **Lord Garmadon**: supreme bad guy and Ninjago's resident villain. Yup, that's me. Some people call me Garmy. But you can call me . . . *Garmadon*.

I'm guessing you picked up this book because you have an unquenchable thirst for conquering things. That's cool. You've come to the right place. I'm here to help you conquer things the Garmadon way. See, when I'm not making mayhem, I like to be a mentor. A teacher. A bad-guy guru.

Does that surprise you? It shouldn't. Villains have our soft sides. Hey, we like to party. We like to get down with our bad selves. It just so happens we also like to conquer — *a lot*. And with this book — plus a little inspiration from me, Lord Garmadon — you can conquer your wildest dreams.

Just don't mess up, or I'll have to fire you out of a volcano. **(Ha! I'm kidding.*)**

*I'm not kidding. Seriously, don't mess up.

IT'S GOOD TO BE BAD

A lot of people ask me, "Garmadon, how come you're so good at being *bad*?" That's an excellent question. I'd have to say, it's just what I do. Everyone has their something that makes them special. Some people are good at crunching numbers. Other people are good at chess or teaching Pilates classes.

> I'LL NEVER FORGET THE DAY I SAID TO MYSELF, "GARMADON, YOU'RE GOING TO USE YOUR TWO EXTRA ARMS, YOUR FIERY DRIVE, AND YOUR SMOLDERING BAD-GUY LOOKS TO CONQUER THE WORLD."

As for me? I happened to get bitten by an evil snake, grow two extra arms, and develop an insatiable desire for conquering. Being bad literally runs in my blood. And that's a good thing! Whether it's numbers or exercise or the snake thing, it's what you do with your *something* that makes you special.

OVERLORD ADVICE:
What's your special something?

FRIENDS AND FOES

Of course, when your goal is world domination, people will either love you or hate you. The trick is to not let the haters get you down. Here are just a few examples of the friends and foes I deal with on an everyday basis.

SHARK ARMY HENCHMEN

The biggest allies in my conquering corner are my reliable band of henchmen. They are all strong, obedient, and shark themed. Why? Because nothing strikes fear into the hearts of unsuspecting civilians like *sharks*.

Friends

SECRET NINJA FORCE

And my biggest nemeses are the Secret Ninja Force. They are Just. The. Worst. Always thwarting me from conquering Ninjago City with

their dragon mechs and their weird bug mechs and their other not-as-cool-as-shark-themed mechs. I mean, look at them. They don't even have cool suits!

Foes!

THE GREEN NINJA

To make matters worse, the leader of the Secret Ninja Force is the Green Ninja, who also happens to be my son, La-loyd. (Yes, it's pronounced just like that. With extra emphasis on the first *L*. I should know — I named him.)

But I didn't realize the Green Ninja was my son until just recently. Now things are *awkward*.

IT'S PRONOUNCED *LLOYD*, DAD. THE FIRST *L* IS SILENT.

Family Foes!

KOKO AND WU

And then there are the family members who turn
out to be foes. Take my brother, Master Wu, and my
ex-wife, Koko. All these years, Master Wu has been
teaching Lloyd to fight against me. Something about
not wanting him to follow in my conquering footsteps,
blah, blah, blah.

News flash: Conquering is cool!
Guess they didn't get the memo.

GET YOUR CONQUER ON

But enough about them. You opened this book to learn about world domination! So, let me ask you something: Are you ready to be bad? I mean, *really* bad?

Are you ready to do something wrong and maybe a little bit wicked?

If the answer is YES, then follow me. It's time to get this show on the road, conquering style!

WHAT WOULD YOU LIKE TO CONQUER TODAY?

GARMADON'S GREATEST CONQUERING HITS

Nothing gives me that bad-boy pride like checking something off my "to-conquer" bucket list. And when conquering is your game, there's always something new to take down! Check out some of my greatest feats.

SUCCESSFULLY CONQUERED!

I CAN SHAKE MY OWN HAND AND LOOK GOOD DOING IT.

LOOKING VILLAIN-Y

When I first got bitten by that evil snake and grew two extra arms, I was a little freaked out. But I learned to embrace my new evil looks with all four arms. That's when I got the upper hands on all the conquering competition.

SUCCESSFULLY CONQUERED!

VOLCANIC LIVING

Every bad guy needs a cool headquarters. And you know what's cooler than cool? *HOT*. As in, I made my headquarters inside an active volcano. All the other bad guys in town are super-jealous that I *own* a volcano.

SUCCESSFULLY CONQUERED!

EVERY URBAN AREA EXCEPT NINJAGO CITY

Someone should tell all those other cities they need a Secret Ninja Force to protect them. Oh, wait. Too late. I conquered them. Ha-ha!

GARMADON'S CONQUERING BUCKET LIST

Of course, with every victory there comes a chance of defeat. My conquering bucket list remains irritatingly short one item: *Ninjago City*.

WHY NINJAGO CITY?

I'm just going to let my walls down for a second and tell you why I want to conquer Ninjago City so badly. About sixteen years ago, I lost something there that was very special to me. Something I never should have given up . . .

ARE YOU SURE THERE'S NOT ANY OTHER SORT OF CONNECTION YOU HAVE TO NINJAGO CITY?

See, I had this guitar in college that I stupidly traded for a jacket or something. Worst mistake ever. That's why I want to conquer Ninjago City.

It definitely doesn't have anything to do with my son, La-loyd. Or the family I left behind in Ninjago City sixteen years ago. You know, the family I didn't even remember I had until just now.

NOPE. JUST THE GUITAR THING.

CONQUERING 1, 2, 3

It's so incredibly easy to conquer Ninjago City; I seriously don't know how my troops and I haven't been successful yet. I mean, look at this. How easy is this? All I have to do is:

1. CLIMB TO THE TOP OF THE NINJAGO TOWER.

2. GET COMFY IN THE MAYOR'S CHAIR.

3. AND PLANT MY CONQUERING FLAG.

MANAGING YOUR CONQUERING EXPECTATIONS

So what's on your conquering bucket list? Before you go all super-villain and say, "the world," you should probably manage your conquering expectations. It's highly unlikely you'll conquer the world. But you can conquer, say, your homework. See, it's all about perspective. Go ahead and quote me on that. "It's all about perspective." Copyright: Garmadon.

DON'T TRY THIS AT HOME

I know how impressive this all looks. And that's because it *is* impressive. But I got bitten by an evil snake and developed super-conquering powers. You need to use *your* superpowers to conquer what *you* want to be the best at.

YOUR CONQUERING EXPERTISE

Are you good at math? Writing? Throwing dodgeballs and taking names? Then conquer it up! Ace that test. Slay that essay. *Win that game.* Remember, it's what you *do* with your special talent that counts.

OVERLORD ADVICE:
What's something you'd like to conquer?

QUIZ: DO YOU HAVE WHAT IT TAKES TO BE A CONQUEROR?

Entering the field of conquering can be daunting. Luckily for you, I've developed *Garmadon's Quiz for Determining If You Have What It Takes to Be a Conqueror.* Also copyright: Garmadon. Who knows? Today you could conquer your homework, tomorrow . . . the world!*

1. When you wake up in the morning, are you eager to hop out of bed?

2. When you get to school, are you pumped up and ready to hit the books?

3. When you take a test, do you settle for nothing less than an A+?

*But seriously, not the world. Leave that to the professionals.

4. If you have to run a mile for gym class, do you run a little bit extra just because you can?

5. At home, do you finish your chores, your homework, *and* eat your brussels sprouts?

6. Are you always the first in line for everything? Like lunch? The movies? The ice-cream truck . . . even if there are little kids waiting there, too?

7. Would you describe your personality as confident and driven with a little bit of evil mastermind?

8. Do you have a map in your bedroom with pushpins on the places you'll conquer one day?

9. Do you have an evil theme song?

10. Do you love . . . sharks?

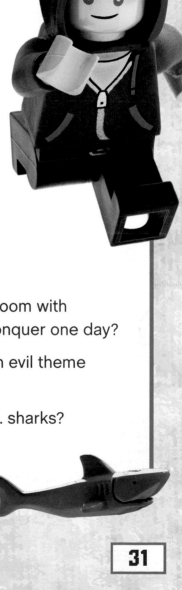
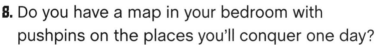

CONQUEROR QUIZ ANSWERS

If you answered *Yes* to three questions or fewer: Hmmmm. You don't really have that "world-domination" chutzpah. Maybe you should pick up a copy of Master Wu's book *Ninjanuity.* I hear it's chock-full of peace and harmony mumbo jumbo.

If you answered *Yes* to five questions: All right, now that's a "can-do" attitude right there! You're good at life and at school, and you know it! Today, you will conquer both.

If you answered *Yes* to seven questions: Wow. You're getting the hang of this villain business. Stay on this path, and one day, you might conquer your town!

If you answered *Yes* to ten questions: Hmmm. Perhaps I was mistaken. Maybe you *will* conquer the world. Have you considered making a career of being an evil villain? I'm always looking for a new General Number One.

GARMADON'S WORDS OF WISDOM

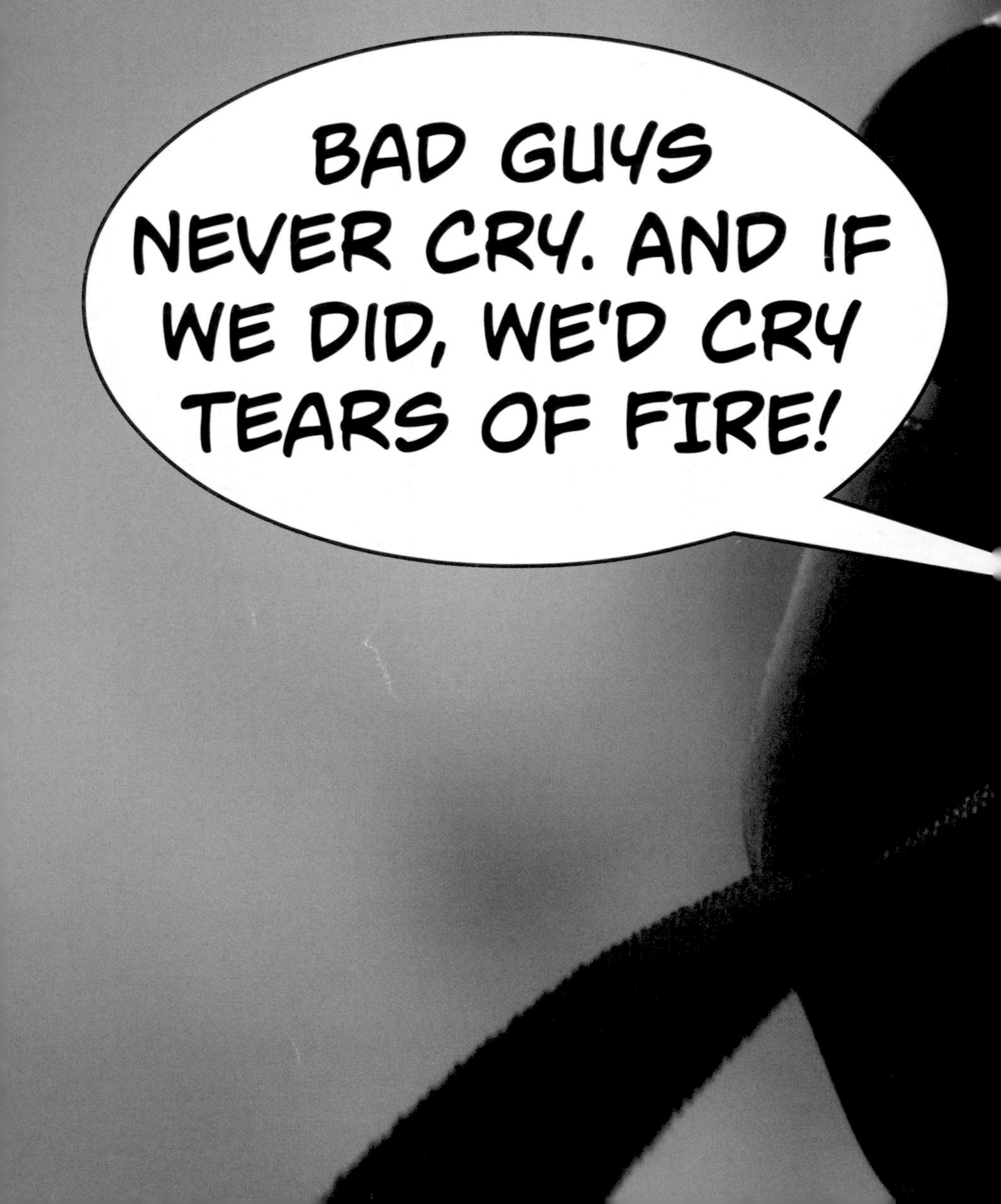

GARMADON'S GUIDE TO

GETTING YOUR CONQUER ON

LIVING LARGE

So you've decided what you want to conquer. Excellent. Now it's time to put that plan into action. There are certain things every good bad guy needs in order to get their conquer on.

Fiery Command Room

Underwater Docking Station ⤴

SMOLDERING HOT LAIR

A personalized home base is the perfect place to kick back, relax, and plot your next conquering challenge. I decided long ago to build mine in a volcano. It's just the right combination of intimidating and sweltering.

Engineering ⤴

LOYAL HENCHMEN

Henchmen are another key necessity. And my henchmen are off the hook. As in, fishhook. (Ha, see what I did there?)

I've invested a ton of money in my henchmen's suits. They have crab suits. Jellyfish suits. Pufferfish suits. SHARK suits. (Maybe I've spent too much money on suits.)

GARMADON LIKES OUR NEW PLANS! HIGH-FIVE!

IT NERDS

A bad guy can't stay ahead of the conquering curve all by himself. Meet my IT Nerds. These nerdy-looking nerd-nerds are the ones who come up with my killer gadgets and sweet rides.

THE SEARCH FOR GENERAL NUMBER ONE

I'm always searching for my perfect General Number One. I'm not sure why. I mean, it's not like I have a gaping hole in my life left by the son I never got to spend quality time with. But for some reason, none of my henchmen ever live up to my General Number One expectations.

SUPER SHARK MECHS

Awesome mechs are crucial for setting that "I'm going to take over the world" tone. Picture this: It's a sunny day at Ninjago Beach. The breeze is blowing. Music is playing. An ice-cream truck sells ice cream to cute little kids.

Suddenly, a dorsal fin pokes above the water. Ominous music starts to play. The ground shakes. A crazy shark mech rises out of the sea, ready to strike! Citizens cry out and run away! *Lord Garmadon has arrived*.

Now *that's* an entrance!

43

BAD GUY SKILLZ

When all else fails, a villain must be ready to get down and dirty. Which means mastering sick dark-ninja skills.

"THE MISO SLAP"

"THE TIGHTY-WHITEY"

HOW WOULD YOU GET YOUR CONQUER ON?

Time for another trademarked Garmadon Conquering Quiz. Choose one option from each column of the grids below to determine your Henchmen Outfits, Bad Guy Skillz, and Giant Mech.

HENCHMEN OUTFITS

Double	Bellied	Unicorns
Fire	Clawed	Polar Bears
Rainbow	Tailed	Dragons
Fuzzy	Headed	Lobsters

OVERLORD ADVICE:
Now that's what I call *PIZZAZZ*.

BAD GUY SKILLZ

Spinning	Tornado	of Enlightenment
Flaming	Daggers	of Lava
Crazy	Dance	of Lasers
Powerful	Kicks	of Doo-Doo

GIANT MECH

Ultra	Feisty	Jaguar
Mega	Snarling	Parrot
Supreme	Snapping	Dinosaur
Tiny	Dancing	Turtle

GARMADON'S WORDS OF WISDOM

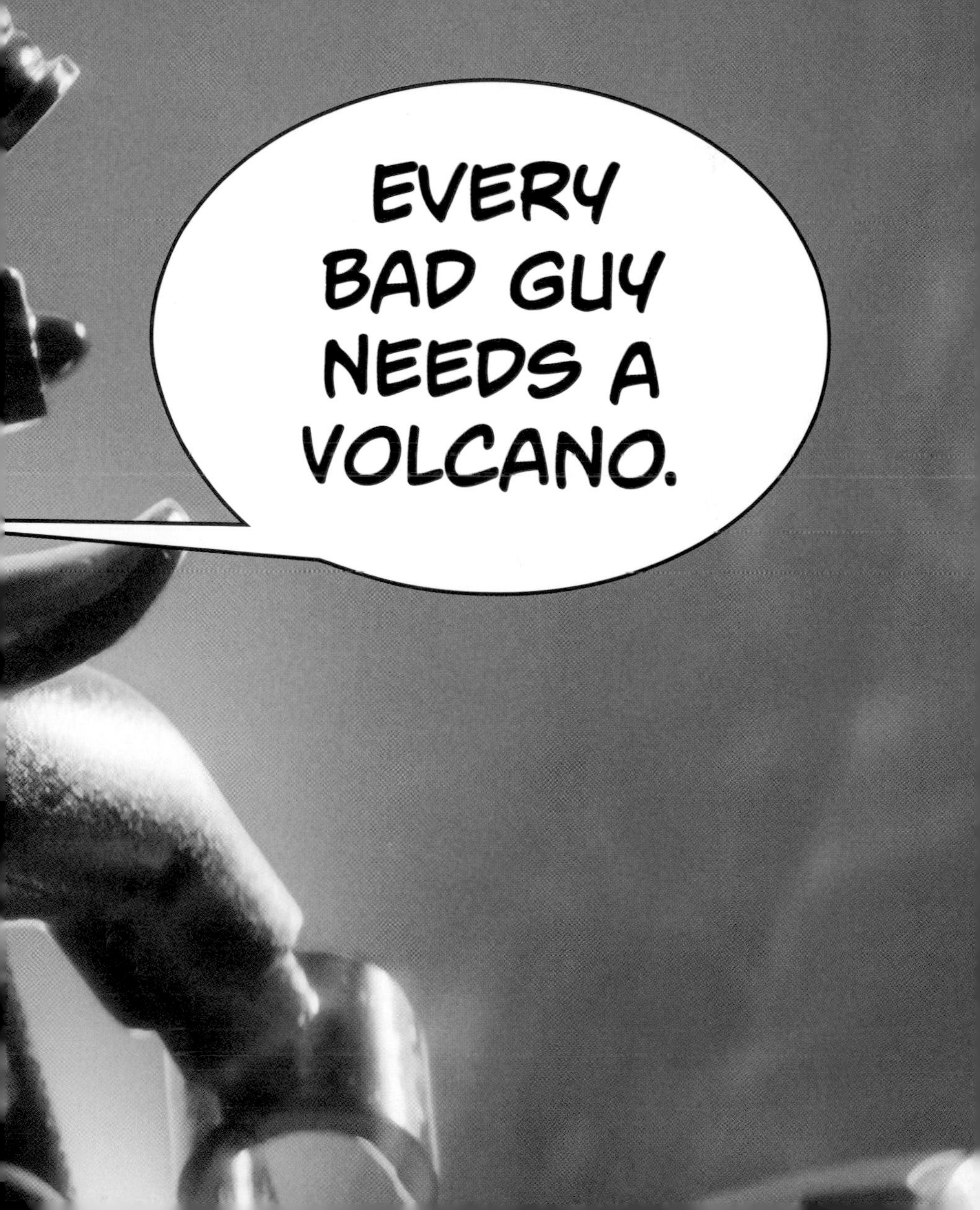

GARMADON'S GUIDE TO

DRESSING
FOR SUCCESS

SUIT UP

If you're looking to conquer your wildest dreams, then you need to look the part. You want a signature style that shows you're not messing around.

Now, I'm going to let my walls down here again for a second. I wasn't always so confident about my smoldering bad-guy looks. When I first got bitten by that snake and grew two extra arms, I was . . . I can't believe I'm saying this . . . *embarrassed*.

But remember how I taught you that it's all about perspective? I had to really *own* my two extra arms. Now I know that I look fetchingly evil no matter how I'm rolling!

WORK CLOTHES

This is how I would dress for success in the normal world. Like, if I was working a boring nine-to-five job in a cubicle with no sunlight somewhere. I'd still *own* it like the conqueror I was born to be.

WHEN YOU HAVE TWO EXTRA ARMS, TAILORING IS CRUCIAL.

PLAYCLOTHES

And this is how I dress when I am getting my conquer on.

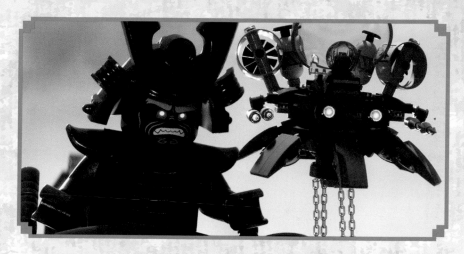

EVIL VILLAIN

Tall, dark, and evil is totally my thing. Aw, yeah. Can you feel the power? I can.

In these threads, the camera adds ten pounds . . . of awesome!

SHARK MECH

Nothing strikes fear in the hearts of innocent beachgoers like a giant shark mech stomping out of the ocean.

OVERLORD ADVICE:
What style conquers your closet?

HAMMERHEAD SHARK MECH

When the normal shark look just isn't enough, it's time to drop the hammerhead shark suit. Oooh. Garma-daddy likey!

Evil Villain Tip: Elliptical-powered mechanics allow you and your enemies to feel the burn!

BORING NINJA SUITS

I guess even the ninja know how to own what makes them special. As in, they know how to own *boring*. Just look at their suits. They're so blah! What are those, primary colors? Are they in preschool? Did they color their gis with crayons? Ugh, so boring.

GARMADON'S TOP TEN TIPS TO DRESSING FOR SUCCESS

10. When in doubt, go with the shark look. Works every time.

9. Dress for your body, not your age. I'm 174 years old. Would you know it by how I dress?

8. Always check out the rear view. Is your shark tail showing?

7. Create a personal look. Have I mentioned sharks are so in right now?

6. Try new things. Like a jellyfish helmet or lobster-claw gloves.

5. Take note of trends . . . and *conquer them.*

4. Quality versus quantity: Choose one mega-weapon accessory and flaunt it.

3. Layer your look. A shark suit topped with a shark mech is always sharp.

2. Tailor outfits to suit your best features, like two extra arms.

1. Black goes with everything.

GARMADON'S WORDS OF WISDOM

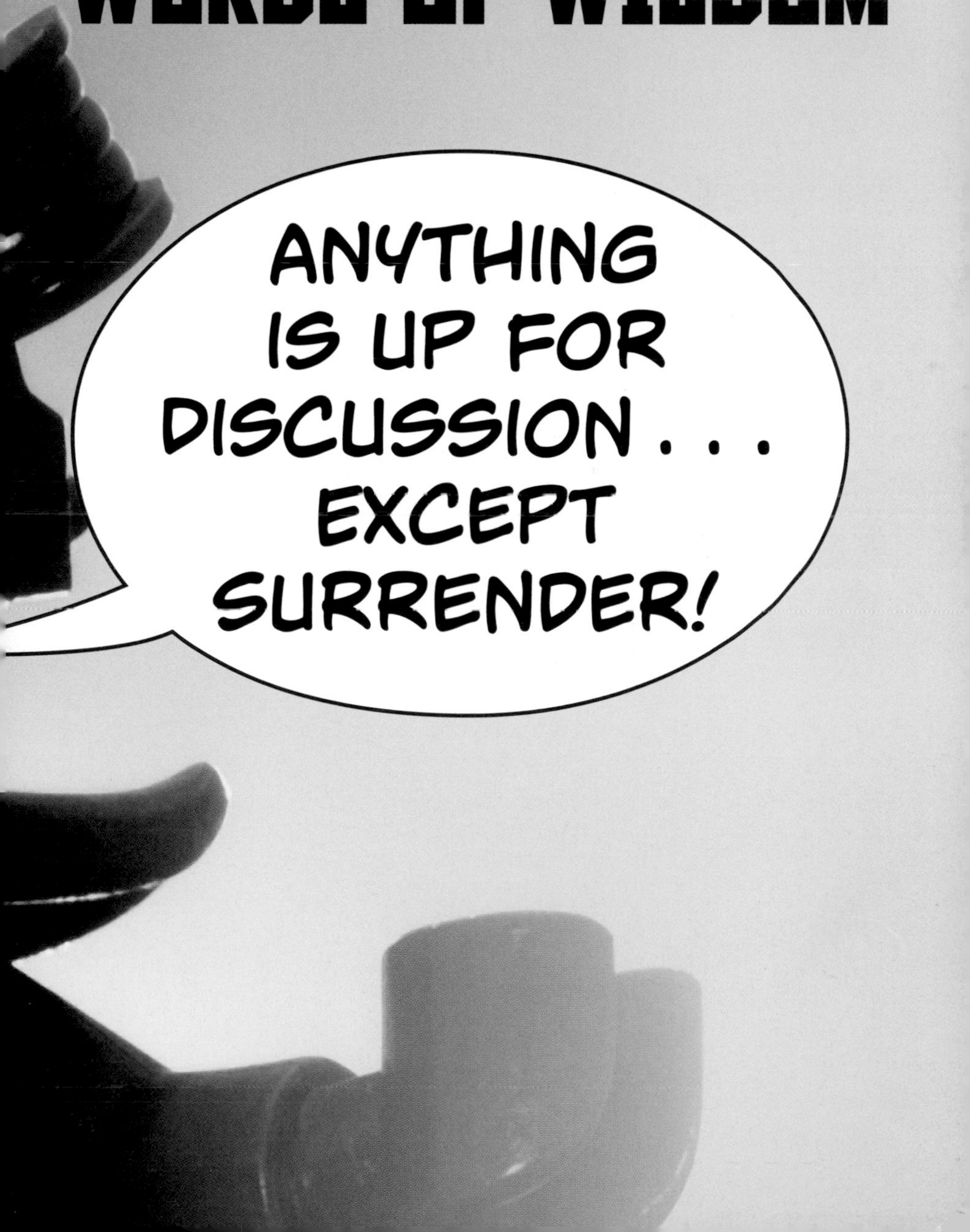

GARMADON'S GUIDE TO

TALKING THE TALK

IT'S ALL ABOUT PRESENTATION

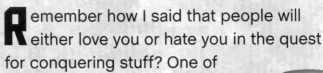

Remember how I said that people will either love you or hate you in the quest for conquering stuff? One of the best ways to bring the haters around is to change their perspective. As an evil villain, I get asked a lot of questions. The trick is to respond in the most upbeat yet vague way possible.

TALKING THE TALK

THE MANIACAL LAUGH

Also key in the life of a villain: the evil laugh. It will make or break you in this industry. Just listen.

TALKING THE TALK

MWA-HA-HA-HA!

GARMADON'S WORDS OF WISDOM

ANYTHING WORTH DOING IS WORTH DOING FAST AND RECKLESSLY.

GARMADON'S GUIDE TO

OVERCOMING OBSTACLES

WHEN THE GOING GETS TOUGH

No one ever said the road to world domination would be smooth. Whether you're conquering school, sports, family, or life, there are going to be challenges along the way. Since I'm an evil villain, my challenges are especially challenge-y. But I don't let that get me down.

BATTLING THE NINJA

For you, an everyday obstacle is probably a bad hair day or a rough morning at school. But for me, everyday obstacles are high stakes. And they usually start with the letter *N* for *Ninja*.

Ugh, the Secret Ninja Force. Have I mentioned they're the worst? Always stopping me from conquering Ninjago City, until that one fateful day . . .

THE ULTIMATE WEAPON

. . . when my son, La-loyd, fired the Ultimate Weapon at me. Can you imagine? He fired it at ME, his papa! The nerve! Someone should have taught that kid some respect when he was little.

Anyway, the joke was on him. The Ultimate Weapon summoned the unstoppable beast. And that creature did my dirty work: taking out the ninja and Ninjago City! I had finally achieved my ultimate conquering goal — Ninjago City was mine! Ha-ha!

UNEXPECTED OBSTACLES

But then, my obstacles became even more intense. You see, my brother, Master Wu, decided to lead the ninja on a mission to get the Ultimate *Ultimate* Weapon. Well, if Wu thought he could use the Ultimate *Ultimate* Weapon to take down the beast and take back Ninjago City, he had another think coming.

WHAT'S HE SAYING? OMELETTE-OMELETTE WEAPON? SOUNDS DELICIOUS. AND QUITE POSSIBLY DANGEROUS.

BROTHER VS. BROTHER!

I had to battle Wu using my dark-ninja skills. The whole time we were fighting, he kept telling La-loyd something about finding his "inner peace" to save Ninjago City. Blah, blah, blah. "Oh, look at me, I'm Master Wu, and today's lesson is something totally boring." Too bad he was so distracted that I totally beat him.

WORKING *WITH* THE NINJA

With Wu gone, the ninja had no choice but to bring *me* along as their master. That was the only way they'd make it through their mission alive. Because the path to the Ultimate *Ultimate* Weapon led through the Forest of Whispers, across the Bridge of Fallen Mentors, and to the Temple of Fragile Foundations.

I know, I was a little surprised to be working *with* the ninja, too. But how else was I supposed to get all my hands on the Ultimate *Ultimate* Weapon? It's not like I was going along with them because I felt somewhat responsible for La-loyd's well-being.

See how well these ninja blend into the shadows? They definitely needed a new mentor.

SKELETON ARMY

Although, I guess there was that moment when I was a little worried if La-loyd was okay as we fought some creepy skeletons . . .

WEIRD. THE BAD-GUY SIDE OF ME SAYS TO DO NOTHING, BUT THE FATHER SIDE OF ME SAYS I SHOULD HELP HIM.

OUT-OF-LEFT-FIELD OBSTACLES

But once I got my hands on the Ultimate *Ultimate* Weapon, I thought my obstacles were all behind me. All I needed to do was

THIS. ISN'T. WHAT. I. WAS. EXPECTING.

use the Ultimate *Ultimate* Weapon and Ninjago City would be mine forever!

Turns out, I was wrong. Very wrong. As in, I got eaten by a cat wrong.

OBSTACLES YOU DIDN'T EVEN KNOW YOU HAD

But you know what? All those challenges turned out to be leading me to one giant obstacle I didn't even know I had. I've seen a lot of crazy stuff as a super-villain. And I've

YOU, YOU SAVED ME, SON. FROM THE CAT.

DAD, ARE YOU . . . CRYING?

NO. IT'S JUST THAT — I'M KIND OF ALLERGIC TO CATS.

done a lot of bad things. Really bad things. Things that were so bad, they were a little bit ghastly.

But I never realized that the biggest, baddest thing I'd ever done was not being there for La-loyd all along.

SOMETIMES, YOU MEET YOUR SOUL MATE ON THE BATTLEFIELD, AND IT'S LOVE AT FIRST FIGHT.

GARMADON'S GUIDE TO

THE FAMILY THAT CONQUERS TOGETHER STICKS TOGETHER

O kay, I'm letting the walls down again here. To teach you my next conquering lesson, you're going to need a little backstory. So here you go. I give you . . . the Garmadon family tree. You can see that martial arts runs strong in my family. You could call it the glue that binds us.

My brother, Wu, and me.

I've always loved Koko's fire.

Our wedding.

Our little conquering family.

LOVE IS A BATTLEGROUND

I remember the first time I ever laid eyes on La-loyd's mom, Koko. Back then, she went by her ninja warrior name — Lady Iron Dragon. I was pillaging a peaceful village with my

skeleton army when I spotted this beautiful warrior queen from across a crowded battlefield. She was fighting for good *and* looking great doing it. Even as she decimated my forces, I couldn't take my eyes off her. I was speechless. It was love at first fight!

SEPARATE PATHS

I thought Koko and I would conquer the world together. Until, one day, we came across *Ninjago City*. I told Koko I wanted to build our son's future on the ashes of that fine city. That's when she realized the life of a conqueror wasn't the life she wanted for La-loyd . . .

I could have changed . . .

. . . but I didn't. And before I knew it, she was gone. And so was La-loyd.

REBUILDING YOUR FAMILY

Whew, that was heavy! Okay, backstory over. But here's the point of all that mushy-gushy sentiment. The family that conquers together sticks together. Those conquering goals need to be the same. I should have realized keeping Koko and La-loyd in my life was more important than . . . I can't believe I'm saying this . . . *conquering.*

I WISH YOU WEREN'T MY FATHER!

And as it turns out, rebuilding your family can be a whole lot harder than conquering things.

SAY WHAT?

When I first discovered La-loyd was the Green Ninja, he said he wished I wasn't his father. Talk about disrespect! My brother, Wu, must have taught him that.

I'M SURE YOU MEAN THAT AS A COMPLIMENT, BUT IT'S A WEIRD THING TO SAY.

FATHER-SON BONDING

It took a lot to earn back La-loyd's trust. I had to totally change my perspective and do things I'd never done before. *Dad* things. Like picking up the phone and calling just to say hi.

STICKING TOGETHER

But in a way, doing dad things felt good. Like it was something I was meant to do, maybe even more than conquering the world. Maybe I was supposed to conquer . . . being a dad.

GARMADON'S WORDS OF WISDOM

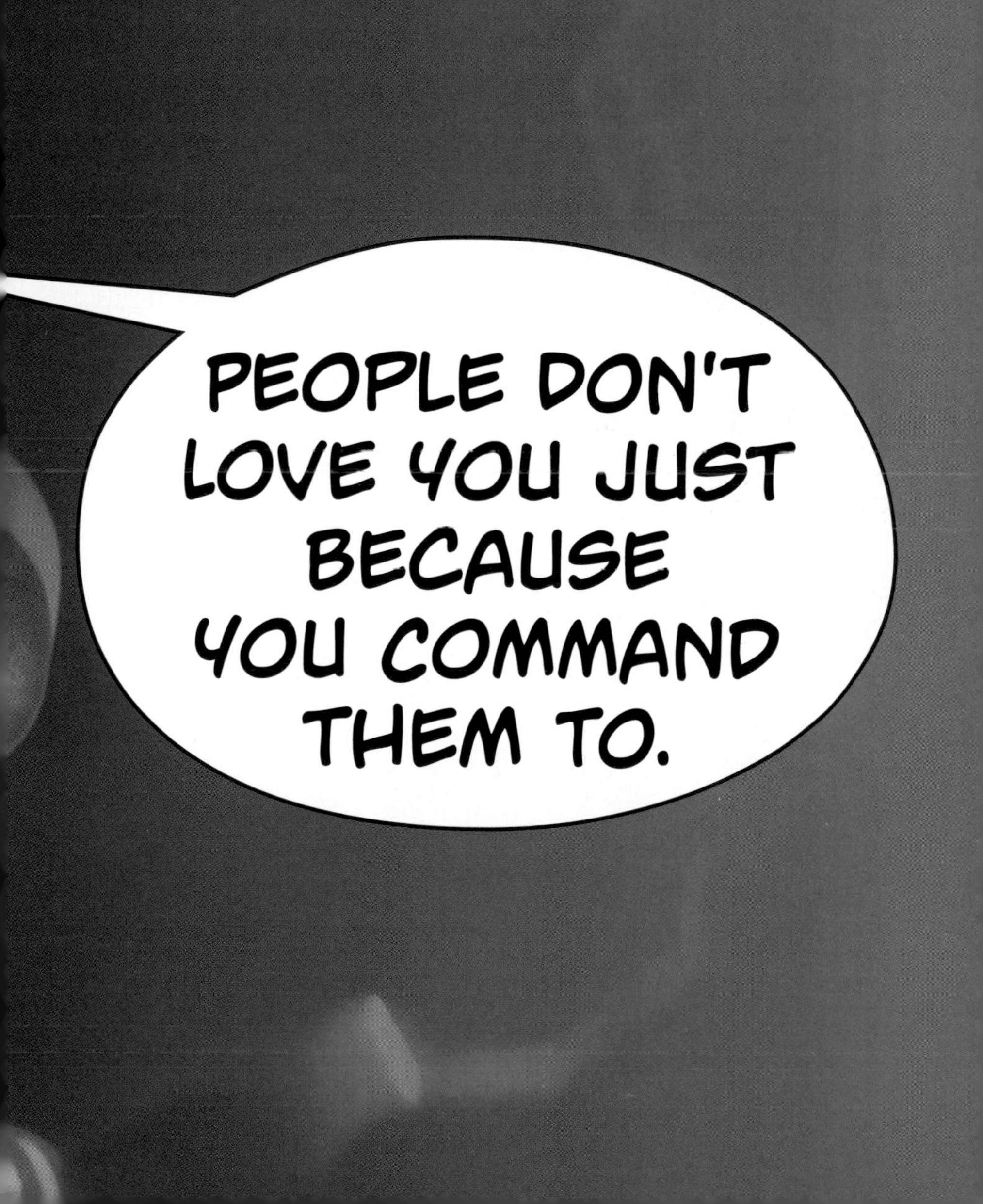

GARMADON'S
GUIDE TO

FINDING YOUR INNER PIECE

KNOWING WHAT YOU WANT (WHAT YOU REALLY, TRULY WANT)

My brother, Wu, is always talking about "inner peace, harmony, and self-reflection." The usual "oh, look at me, I'm a goody-two-shoes martial artist" stuff. Blah, blah, blah, whatever. Also, his beard is weird.

But I guess he might kind of, sort of, have a point. Even bad guys need to do a self-assessment every now and again to make sure what they're conquering is truly what they want to conquer. All these years, I kept defeating city after city, but I always felt like I was missing *something*.

FINDING YOUR INNER PIECE

SOMETIMES YOU'VE GOT TO SMILE

Then, after working together with those ninja and fighting alongside La-loyd, I started to get a whole new perspective on things. And suddenly, something weird happened. I felt . . . happy. At first, I thought maybe my old General Number Ones had poisoned us or something. But La-loyd told me it was a good thing.

THE INNER PIECE

That's when I realized: My brother, Wu, wasn't talking about finding "inner peace." He meant inner *piece*. As in, the thing that completes you.

Ever since I got bitten by that snake, I thought conquering completed me. But it turned out, I felt most complete with my son by my side. My inner piece was La-loyd all along. Who knew?

Of course, there was a second where I almost messed things up:

LA-LOYD, YOU'VE GROWN UP TO BE AN AMAZING NINJA WARRIOR. WILL YOU COME BACK TO NINJAGO CITY WITH ME AS FATHER AND . . . GENERAL NUMBER ONE?

WHEN PEOPLE LOOK AT YOU, THEY SEE A MONSTER. BUT *I* KNOW THAT YOU JUST FEEL SCARED AND ALONE. I KNOW HOW THAT FEELS. AND I KNOW NOW THAT I'LL NEVER HAVE BALANCE IN MY LIFE IF I DON'T HAVE YOU. I FORGIVE YOU. I JUST NEED MY DAD.

But in the end, La-loyd helped me fix things. He even rescued me from being eaten by a giant monster. Now that's father-son bonding.

GARMADON'S WORDS OF WISDOM

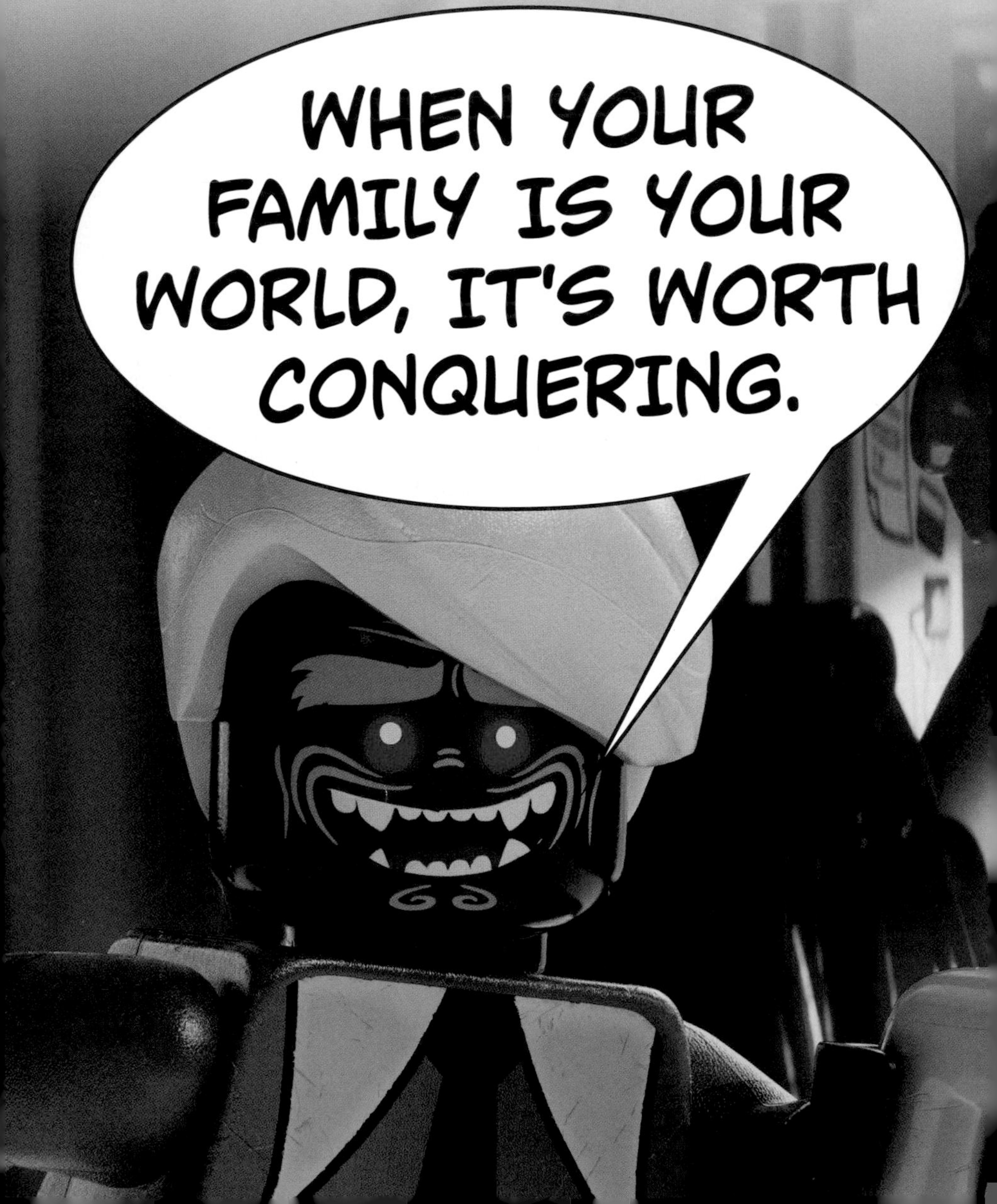

GARMADON'S GUIDE TO

IEVING YOU CONQUERING GOALS

THE MORAL OF THE STORY

So, I guess the moral of the story is, when you start writing a guide to world domination, you should probably decide if you're writing a guide to actual world domination. Because sometimes you *think* you know what you want to conquer . . .

THIS IS FUN, RIGHT? WE'RE HAVING FUN? I CAN'T TELL.

. . . when what you *really* want to conquer is something entirely different, like rebuilding your family. Brick by brick. Piece by piece. Using all four arms.

WHAT ARE YOUR CONQUERING GOALS?

Time for another trademarked Garmadon Conquering Quiz, courtesy of me, Lord Garmadon. Answer the questions below to find out what your ultimate conquering goals are.

1. Who are the most important people to you? If you could conquer one thing with them today, what would it be?

2. What are your dreams for the future? How will you conquer them?

3. What do you love doing? Are there ways you could do it better?

4. What is a skill you'd like to pursue? How will you master it?

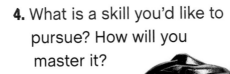

5. Is there anything you're afraid of? How will you overcome that fear?

6. If you could help someone else conquer their dreams, who would it be and how would you help them?

7. Who are the people that help you to achieve your goals? How will you let them know they're special today?

8. If you could make one difference in the world, what would it be? How would you do it?

9. What's something you could conquer right here, right now?

10. How will you keep being the best possible you every day?

GARMADON'S
WORDS OF WISDOM

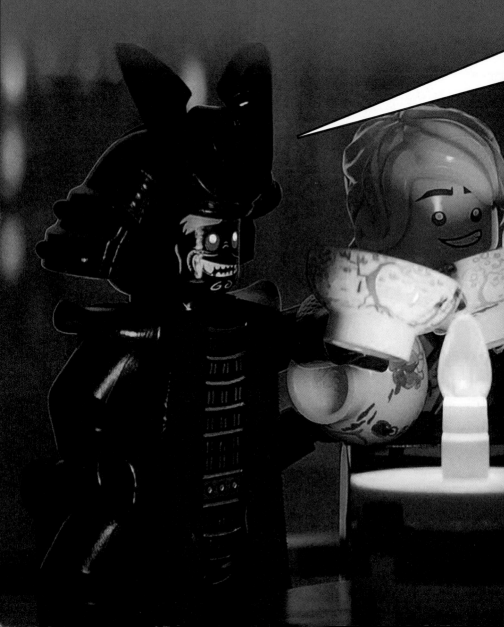

VILLAIN OUT

So there you have it. My guide to conquering your dreams, whatever those dreams may be. And I have to say, for a rookie conqueror, you did pretty well. I'm impressed. No, seriously, I am. At least I didn't have to fire you out of a volcano. We shared some laughs along the way. Cried a few tears of fire. And I think we all learned an important lesson. Conquering your dreams is totally possible. Just make sure you're out to conquer the right ones for you. Hey, that's pretty catchy. I think I'll trademark that. "Make sure you're out to conquer the right dreams for you."
— Copyright: Garmadon.

BAD GUY OUT.

GET YOUR CONQUER ON EVERY DAY

The conquering fun doesn't have to stop just because this book is over. Here are some mastermind ways to get your conquer on every day, every way.

1. Start each day with a to-do list, and then get cracking! There's nothing more satisfying than crossing something off your conquering list.

2. Share your dreams with someone special, like your parents or best friends. They can help you reach them!

3. Pick something new to master every month, and then practice, practice, practice. Villains don't become successful overnight, you know.

4. Make a dream journal, as in, your dreams for the future. Write about them now so you can read about them once they're reality.

5. Take a minute each day to tell your family why they're special to you. They're the biggest allies in your conquering corner, after all.

THE

BUILD YOUR
THE LEGO®
NINJAGO®
MOVIE™
LIBRARY!